© **Copyright SSJH GROUP Ltd 202:** **^II rights reserved.**

The content contained within reproduced, duplicated or tra written permission from the auth

Under no circumstances will any blame or legal responsibility be held against the publisher, or author, for any damages, reparation, or monetary loss due to the information contained within this book. Either directly or indirectly. You are responsible for your own choices, actions, and results.

Legal Notice:

This book is copyright protected. This book is only for personal use. You cannot amend, distribute, sell, use, quote or paraphrase any part, or the content within this book, without the consent of the author or publisher.

Disclaimer Notice:

Please note the information contained within this document is for educational and entertainment purposes only. All effort has been executed to present accurate, up to date, and reliable, complete information. No warranties of any kind are declared or implied. Readers acknowledge that the author is not engaging in the rendering of legal, financial, medical or professional advice. The content within this book has been derived from various sources. Please consult a licensed professional before attempting any techniques outlined in this book.

By reading this document, the reader agrees that under no circumstances is the author responsible for any losses, direct or indirect, which are incurred as a result of the use of the information contained within this document, including, but not limited to, — errors, omissions, or inaccuracies.

365 Positive Affirmations For Black Men

Daily Affirmations for BIPOC Men to Boost Self-Love, Healing, Growth in Money & Success, & Overcoming Obstacles by Sam Shaw

Introduction

For far too long black men have been made to see themselves as inferior or grossly lacking certain criteria that distinguish people for success. It is appalling that we have bought into these lies that make us see ourselves as less than, so we strive in vain to attain false beauty standards set by society while we neglect the power in our own identity. It is impossible to live successful and happy lives without possessing confidence in our abilities. Therefore, it is time black men took a stand against all forms of systemic marginalisation set up to relegate them and all they stand for.

To do this, certain harmful ideologies need to be flushed out. These are ideologies that paint false pictures of incompetence and inadequacy in the minds of black men about themselves which hamper their ability to reach full potential. Our thoughts are very powerful and sometimes, even powerful enough to affect the way we function; negative thoughts can only birth more negativity in our lives. These need to be replaced with values that challenge us to become even better than we already are ought to be embraced.

If you are a black man on a journey of self-realisation and actualisation, then this guide is for you. It is packed with powerful affirmations that will assist you on your journey to becoming a better you as you learn to love yourself for the immensely gifted king that you are, let go of disappointments from your past to find healing within yourself, unlock doors to successful living and overcome all obstacles standing between you and your purpose. Affirmations are known to help reinforce positive thoughts and energy, and consequently, better lifestyle patterns. The affirmations contained in this book are capable of reprogramming your subconscious to inculcate life-giving beliefs and values that can alter the way you see yourself and your capabilities. They will unlock the power you have in your tongue and mind as you begin to attract the positivity that you confess over your life.

It is time to make a daily habit of absorbing values that can transform the way we look at ourselves, that can mould us into the very image of all that we aspire to be and can be passed on to our sons and our sons' sons; the first step begins here.

Chapter 1: SELF LOVE AFFIRMATIONS

1. I am not what the world thinks or says I am, I am an embodiment of excellence and I begin to manifest excellence in all that I do.

2. My body is a sacred temple that is intricately designed and I begin to treat it with the love and acceptance it deserves.

3. My skin is beautiful and it glows with a radiance that causes me to stand out everywhere I go.

4. I am a strong man, I walk with a confident spring in my step and my head is held high with dignity.

5. I embrace the peculiarities that make me who I am.

6. I am not a misfit, I am uniquely built in the reflection of my heritage.

7. I exist, therefore I matter.

8. I deserve to be loved, I deserve to be respected, I deserve to be happy and I begin to treat myself with the love and respect I deserve. I begin to find happiness all around me.

9. I speak positive things into my life, I think positive thoughts about myself and I begin to attract positivity all around me.

10. My will is empowered to walk away from all forms of negative influences around me.

11. I am worthy of love and therefore I allow myself to be vulnerable enough to receive love.

12. I have a wholly beautiful, mind body and soul.

13. I advance each day on my journey to self-love and self-discovery.

14. I find peace, comfort and acceptance within myself.

15. My life is worth living, tomorrow is worth waiting for.

16. I will be kind to myself, I will nurture my mind and feed my spirit.

17. I am the author of my own story and I begin to rewrite its plot to tell a better story of courage, strength and self-actualisation.

18. Even if it doesn't look like it, all things are working together to benefit me in the end.

19. I am a force to be reckoned with, the definition of perfection.

20. I have a voice that needs to be heard, I have a story to tell that needs to be retold throughout history.

21. I refuse to depend on others for my validation, I define my own self-worth.

22. I begin to set healthy boundaries and I receive the strength to adhere to them.

23. I learn from my past as I move on from it, I take charge of my present and I prepare myself for a glorious future.

24. I am priceless, of inestimable value and not everyone deserves access to my personal space.

25. I am not buried under, I am planted and I begin to nurture myself for fruitful growth and expansion.

26. It is okay to decline without creating excuses or trying too hard to explain myself.

27. I am dedicated to learning how to love myself better.

28. I stand out like a shining light and I refuse to dim my light for anyone.

29. I come from a history of survivors, I am a descendant of strength and I reach deep within myself to find the resilience planted in my genes.

30. I celebrate myself and I take pride even in the little victories.

31. I step out of the fear and self-doubt that has held me captive and I begin to share my beauty with the world.

32. I have purpose, my life has meaning, and my existence is valid.

33. People come and people go, some remain a part of my life while others may wish to leave. Through all of this, my self-worth remains the same.

34. I have the power to change whatever I am not comfortable with around me and within me.

35. I am grateful for the boy I left behind and I am proud of the man I am becoming.

36. I love my body and I am thankful for how it was created and what it can do.

37. This day is a gift with limitless possibilities and I as I step out into it, I seize all the opportunities it has to offer me.

38. As I attract positivity in my life, I choose to withhold negativity from others. I exude the positivity that I attract.

39. I look into the mirror and the person I see is a god who gets better with each day.

40. My strength and confidence are renewed daily, my self-esteem is boosted daily and I begin to see myself for the amazon that I am.

41. I am an asset to myself, those around me and the world at large.

42. My hair is a lustrous crown that signifies the royal blood that runs through my veins.

43. There is strength in my determination, wonder in my mind and power in my past.

44. I am proud of my culture and how my experiences have shaped me into a phenomenal black man of excellence.

45. When self-doubt threatens to pull me under, I will look within and remind myself of my true worth, then I will rise above the demons of insecurity.

46. I am beautiful, from the kink and curl in my hair to the graceful stride in my steps.

47. I am confident enough to take off the mask I have been wearing while pretending to be someone else and I will unapologetically exist as who I am.

48. I am intentional about investing in the positive things that bring me joy.

49. I am intentional about blocking all channels that give negativity access to my life.

50. I refuse to take out my frustrations on myself.

51. I see past all paranoid assumptions that foster fear and insecurities in my life and I begin to see things clearly as they really are.

52. I begin to attract like-minded people to form healthy and respectful relationships where I can thrive and find support.

53. I let go of the bitter people in my life to create space for better people to come into my life.

54. I starve my weaknesses and I feed my strengths.

55. I deserve better and I refuse to let my insecurities intimidate me into settling for less.

56. I resist the urge to form an inferiority complex by comparing myself with other people.

57. My happiness comes from deep inside me and it cannot be hampered by factors external to me.

58. I do not live for the validation of people and therefore their criticism cannot kill me.

59. I allow myself to have fun and enjoy life to the fullest.

60. I am at ease with myself and I refuse to be too hard on myself.

61. I fall more in love with the person I am becoming daily.

62. I love and appreciate every part or bulge on my body for its unique beauty.

63. My lips, my nose, and everything about my body is appropriately proportional to my bold and vivacious personality.

64. I am a living, breathing reflection of the strength and excellence that my heritage embodies.

65. Instead of wallowing in self-pity, I choose to turn my losses into wins worth celebrating.

66. I am not a cheap knockoff, I am an original work of art.

67. My opinion of myself carries more weight than the negative opinions of others about me.

68. I will learn how to love myself unconditionally.

69. I am loved, I am chosen and I am cherished.

70. I treat myself with the love and grace that I give to others.

71. I will endure disrespect and humiliation, I will communicate how I would rather be treated.

72. I will not criticise myself for not being who I think I should be, instead I will learn to love who I am.

73. Bad days do not make me an incompetent person, they make me human.

74. I free myself from the need for perfect and I strive instead for self-improvement.

75. I will begin to root for myself the way I would support and encourage a dear friend.

76. I intentionally begin to think positive thoughts about myself first thing when I wake up and last thing before I go to bed.

77. I cultivate the habit of feeling proud of myself.

78. I am deserving of love and I will not beg to be loved.

79. I will not shrink myself for others to feel good about themselves, I will grow the way I was created to.

80. I am grateful that I was created this way, I am wonderfully and beautifully made.

81. I will not let my mind be a bully to my body.

82. I am secure with myself because my self-esteem keeps growing daily.

83. I am creating a beautiful life.

84. My choices are inspired by wisdom from within and they aid me on my journey through life.

85. I am precisely who I need to be and where I need to be in this moment.

86. My whole life radiates the beauty that my soul is made of from within.

87. My life attracts everything good and it gives everything good in return.

88. I am cocooned in self-care and self-appreciation.

89. I appreciate each and every single one of my strengths and I celebrate them with gratitude in my heart.

90. My self confidence remains unshaken even in the face of disappointment.

91. I do not need external factors to complete me, I was created whole and I am enough.

92. My life is amazing and it can only get better from here.

93. I feel comfortable speaking my mind and expressing my feelings.

94. I am not unworthy or all the wonderful things I desire, I deserve all the amazing things my heart desires.

95. I am comfortable in this glowing skin.

96. I will no longer downplay my achievements, I am worthy of every compliment that I receive.

97. I am a valuable addition to society, my life makes a difference.

98. I am courageous and outgoing, my life is an adventure full of surprises.

99. I do my best every day and today's efforts are better than yesterday's efforts.

Chapter 2: HEALING AFFIRMATIONS

1. I am ready to take the final step necessary to begin my healing process.

2. Today I will meet others with kindness and sympathy as a reflection of a healthy inner self.

3. I am patient with myself as I give myself time to heal from past hurt and disappointments.

4. I release myself from the bondage of negative words spoken against me which have shaped the way I see myself.

5. I let go of all the pain and anger I have bottled up inside, I rid myself of all the bitterness that has eaten away at my heart and mind for too long.

6. I forgive myself of past mistakes, I forgive myself in advance all the mistakes of the future and I use them as lessons to propel me forward on my journey through life.

7. My failures will not define me, my disappointments will not discourage me, I refuse to let these cage me.

8. I decide today that I will let old wounds heal, no more ripping off the scabs to relive my pain.

9. Whatever is left of my old wounds can no longer hurt me. Instead I begin to see them as battle scars that declare the victories of battles that I have fought and overcome.

10. I refuse to feed the fear that prevents me from working through my pain, I am fierce enough to face whatever is left of my pain and I am brave enough to move on.

11. I am mature enough to acknowledge my mistakes and I am humble enough to ask for forgiveness from those I have hurt.

12. I am brave enough to show compassion and forgive those who have hurt me, whether they deserve it or not.

13. I feel my pain and I feel my anger but I refuse to let them consume me, instead I process them and I use them to my advantage.

14. I learn to accept things that are out of my control and I give my mind over to peace and tranquillity.

15. I put my health - mental, physical and spiritual above all else as I strive for a healthier life.

16. I entrust myself with the duty to take good care of myself and to maintain a healthy and balanced life.

17. I commit myself to the gradual but effective completion of my healing process.

18. I gather strength from within to endure all the momentary pain I have to endure in order to heal.

19. My body, mind and soul function together in a way that supports a healthy daily living and the actualisation of my goals.

20. Letting go of what is behind me, I look forward to a brighter future filled with love and happiness.

21. I step out of the dark closet I was forced into by heartbreaks from the past and I courageously open my heart to love and trust again.

22. I am OK.

23. I constantly meditate on positivity to rid my mind of all negative thoughts.

24. I restrain myself from projecting the offenses committed against me on others around me who mean well.

25. I am grateful for the gift of life as each new day provides a fresh slate to begin again.

26. I eliminate every form of negative energy around me and I create a safe space for myself where I can heal and thrive.

27. I embrace the kind of lifestyle that supports wellbeing of my mind, body and soul and I begin to make choices that guarantee growth in every area of my life.

28. Every time I meditate of healing, my body responds in kind.

29. I trade all my frustrations, anger and failures for hope, peace and determination.

30. I turn the page on sorrow and pain as I begin a new chapter in my life.

31. I refuse to be a victim of my past. It has no power over me.

32. My determination is geared towards getting healthier and happier day after day.

33. I set my heart free from the prison of unforgiveness.

34. I release my attachment to any and everything that keeps me stuck in my painful past.

35. I am willing to forgive myself even if others withhold forgiveness from me.

36. I am attentive to my body, I know what it needs to heal and I am committed to providing the love and care necessary for its healing.

37. I am full of vitality and strength, I refuse to let anything drain me of my energy.

38. I refuse to be affected by any external negativity that tries to throw me off balance, I am at peace with myself.

39. I am determined to create an environment where my emotions can heal and be vulnerable again.

40. My mind is free from anxiety and my heart is free from worry.

41. I refuse to let depression overwhelm me, my happiness comes from within and it radiates all around me.

42. I am a beneficiary of divine health, sickness will not overpower me.

43. Every cell and organ in my body function as they should to support a healthy lifestyle free of infirmity.

44. I have the strength to let go of every habit that can potentially sabotage my health and quality of life.

45. I choose to adopt a healthier lifestyle and I make choices that prioritise my wellbeing above all else.

46. I possess a healthy mind, healthy emotions, healthy body, healthy hair and healthy skin. My whole life is in great shape.

47. I am not a victim, I am a survivor.

48. I break free from everything that tries to weigh me down.

49. My new experiences will be better and they will outnumber the painful experiences from my past.

50. I refuse to drag any negative piece of my past into my future, I leave what is past in the past and I focus on moving into a future that will compensate me for my past losses.

51. I am grateful for my healthy body and I do all that is within my power to keep it healthy.

52. I give my body and mind all they need to flourish.

53. I forego resentment and I embrace love and peace with all men.

54. I live a healthy life in a healthy body.

55. I choose thoughts of complete wellness.

56. I create an environment for myself where my health can thrive.

57. I block all channels of illness in my life.

58. My mind and body respond positively to nature.

59. Every time I lay down to rest, my body receives all the rejuvenation it needs. When I wake up I am revitalised and reenergised for the day ahead.

60. I say yes to all things that support a whole lifestyle.

61. I receive strength in my mind, body and soul.

62. I have no control over my past therefore cease to condemn myself over past deeds.

63. As I go through my healing process, I look forward to a future where I will be whole.

64. I choose to leave my past behind and dwell fully in my present.

65. I am stronger than I used to be and I will rise from the ashes of my past into a more secure future.

66. I will let it hurt, I will let it bleed and I will let it go for my healing process to be complete.

67. I may not be able to undo the wound, but I have the responsibility to let myself heal.

68. For my healing to begin, I need to stop touching my wounds. I let go and I let healing take its full course.

Chapter 3: SUCCESS AFFIRMATIONS

1. I rise above the limitations that society has set for men like me and I claim my place in the universe as a force to be recognised and respected.

2. I trust in my abilities to attain the heights of success I desire.

3. I am bold enough to step out of my comfort zone to take on more risks take me closer to living a successful life.

4. I begin to make smart decisions that order my steps on the path to successful.

5. I always put my best foot forward and I have the confidence to be seen and heard by those who matter.

6. I welcome into my life positive changes that will help me develop habits that will prepare me for success.

7. I begin to attract an overflow of blessings beyond what my natural abilities deserve.

8. I have enough to become a source of blessing in the lives of others.

9. I exercise the law of attraction which helps me attract the abundance that I meditate on daily.

10. I let go of habits that can hinder successful living.

11. I am a go-getter and I will stop at nothing until I go far beyond my wildest dreams.

12. I am equipped with everything I need to push me up the ladder of success.

13. I possess the solutions to solve problems and the world will seek me out for what I have to offer.

14. Every milestone on my path to success will be my testimony against naysayers.

15. I continually push myself to develop and sharpen my skills, stagnancy is not an option.

16. My success will be the sweetest revenge against those who mocked my dreams and aspirations.

17. My mind is focused and I possess the clarity to create strategies that will transform my vision into reality.

18. I am be patient enough to diligently put in the hard work required to make my dreams come true.

19. The barriers that worked against men like me in the past and kept then from fulfilling their purpose will not hinder me from fulfilling mine.

20. I will become an inspiration to other men and young boys will look up to me as the perfect role model.

21. I begin to get ideas that will take my business to the next level.

22. Whatever I lay my hands on begin to prosper.

23. I receive the foreknowledge to detect unprofitable business and career endeavours.

24. My success is not determined by what the economy says, I experience a lifting up even when there is a casting down for most.

25. My mind is tranquil enough to think clearly and make right decisions even in the midst of pressure.

26. I am surrounded by the right kind of people who will help my destiny.

27. I am surrounded by the right kind of people who will give me good counsel concerning my business or career.

28. I possess the mental and emotional intelligence necessary for navigating through my field of expertise.

29. I have the ability to be satisfied and contented without going beyond my means as I work towards acquiring more.

30. My mind is immune to negative comments which seek to destroy my confidence in myself and what I have to offer.

31. I have the resourcefulness to multiply the work of my hands.

32. I let go of every negative mind-set that may cripple my potential to be successful.

33. I embrace the mind-set and thought pattern of an achiever.

34. I embrace the kind of lifestyle that will recognise and maximise every opportunity that is available to me.

35. I will not sit idly at the risk of letting opportunities pass me by, I step out in faith to seize good things for myself.

36. I am a successful man in all that I do.

37. I have all it takes to establish a successful and thriving business or career.

38. My race does not disqualify me for success, it sets me up for accomplishments.

39. I live a life of comfort and ease.

40. No dream is too big, no goal is too high and no level of success is too unattainable for me.

41. Confession brings about possession therefore I begin to manifest the riches and abundance that I confess over my life daily.

42. The words of my mouth carry weight and as I speak them into the atmosphere, they go out and bring prosperity my way.

43. My mind is sharp enough to make rational decisions that push me closer to the kind of life that I desire.

44. I am abundantly blessed and my blessings multiply daily.

45. I am tougher than any challenge trying to withhold me from my success.

46. I am surrounded by an amazing support system of friends and family who push me towards becoming a more successful version of myself.

47. I have the grace to surpass the achievements of those who have gone before me in my career or line of business.

48. As long as there is breath in my lungs, there is room to chase my dreams and achieve all that I set out to accomplish.

49. I deserve to be financially independent and I will pursue my dreams until I can afford the quality of life I desire.

50. I am a confidently step into my world of opportunities, recognising which ones to pursue and which ones to let go.

51. I overflow with creativity and good ideas.

52. Momentary setbacks will not discourage me from moving forward in my pursuit of prosperity.

53. I will celebrate every milestone as an encouragement to keep pushing forward.

54. I will not compromise my determination for a successful life.

55. I am committed to equipping myself with the necessary skills that will aid my pursuit of a successful career or a thriving business.

56. I will enjoy the process of growth and learning leading up to the achievement of my dreams.

57. I have everything I need to live a life of prosperity and abundance.

58. I begin to live like my future blessings are a reality.

59. My daydreams about prosperity transform from mere fantasies to goals that are achievable.

60. I consume positive energy which helps me maintain a centred and balanced life.

61. I can do all things that I set my mind and heart to achieve.

62. I will not be easily dissuaded from fulfilling my purpose in life.

63. I block out every distraction threatening to take my eyes off my goals.

64. My mind is brilliant and it offers me brilliant ideas whenever I need them.

65. My determination to succeed is renewed daily because I will continue to dwell on things that inspire me to be successful.

66. I will work hard at everything that I do and I will reap the benefits of my hard work.

67. I begin to address myself as a person worthy of honour and respect.

68. I overcome every fear that tries to let opportunities slip through my hands.

69. I chase my dreams relentlessly, pausing only to celebrate milestones.

70. My goals are not unrealistic and I am not aiming too high. I will not quit until my dreams come to pass.

71. I am not too timid to pursue the creative ideas that my mind offers me.

72. All the help and assistance I need to bring my dreams to fruition will be made available to me.

73. My mouth will speak the right words to the right people to help speed up my journey to success.

74. I will fit perfectly into a lifestyle of affluence.

75. I will not be too lazy to make the sacrifices needed to live a successful life.

76. As a strong and successful man, I have the discipline to work diligently.

77. I possess the wisdom and grace to deal with the most difficult clients and customers and make them satisfied with my services.

78. I am empowered beyond my natural abilities.

79. Doors of opportunities and blessings will be open wide unto me.

80. I move from breakthrough to breakthrough.

81. My mind will continue to yield profitable strategies for me to advance my plans for success.

82. I am not afraid of a little competition on the road to success.

83. Every day, I discover new and exciting ways to pursue and accomplish my dreams.

84. I work well under pressure and my mind remains focused on the achievement of my goals.

85. I choose to be intentional about succeeding.

86. If the world refuses to create a system that can empower me, I will create my own path to success.

87. Every discouragement is an encouragement to work harder and let my success speak for me.

88. I count my blessings daily and I am grateful for my progress so far.

89. I will not settle for merely dreaming about success, I will dare myself to go out and work for it.

90. I will not overlook the opportunities for success hidden beneath my mistakes. .

91. I can and I will. I have the ability to accomplish whatever I am determined to do.

92. I will consistently work for my financial independence.

93. I will raise my energy to the standard of success that I desire.

94. I will not abandon my pursuit of a better life, I will complete whatever I begin.

95. If success doesn't come to me, I will step out of my comfort zone and I will go to it.

96. I will abandon my fears and I will push myself to do the things I never imagined that I could do.

97. I hold myself in high esteem because I was destined for success.

98. I begin to manifest all the ideas of success that I have conceived in my mind.

99. I will constantly evaluate my daily routine to examine habits and patterns I need to trade for more productive ones.

Chapter 4: OVERCOMING OBSTACLES AFFIRMATIONS

1. Obstacles in my way are not barriers to achieving my dreams, they are hurdles to be surmounted on the journey to my dreams.

2. I rid myself of all emotional blocks that can get in the way of my peace of mind.

3. I promise myself to get back up with even more determination if I stumble on the way to success.

4. This is the confirmation I have been waiting for to get up from my defeat and try again.

5. No challenge is too intimidating for me to back down.

6. Every setback I experience is nothing but another lesson in my success story.

7. My mind is protected from all negative blockers that may try to deter me from forging ahead achieving my vision.

8. I refuse to allow the setbacks of today define the possibilities of tomorrow.

9. I defy all odds set against me by overcoming pitfalls constructed by society for men like me.

10. I push back against any adversary that chooses to stand in my way.

11. External factors cannot quench the fire of my resilience.

12. Obstacles in my way will fall to my feet as stepping stones to my destination.

13. Hard times will not define me, instead, the story will be told of how I conquered my fears and overcame my hardships.

14. I am equipped with everything I need to weather storm on the horizon.

15. Nothing is strong enough to keep me from achieving my goals.

16. I am a survivor and no obstacle can keep me under.

17. No matter what comes my way, I continue to persevere along the path of success.

18. I begin to overcome all the obstacles that have knocked me down in the past.

19. I believe in my ability to stand strong even in the face of adversity.

20. Despite the numerous obstacles in my way, I will leave a legacy of determination and courage behind.

21. I confidently confront new inhibitions with the courage to overthrow them.

22. I am adequately inspired and motivated to always forge ahead in my pursuits.

23. I cultivate courage and resilience in my mind and body as a take on new challenges in my journey through life.

24. I will not be tempted to quit just because others around me are throwing in the towel.

25. My strong determination for success will be a source of inspiration to others struggling with thoughts of giving up.

26. I see all my challenges as potential victories.

27. I will not let the fear of failure keep me from attempting to pass the test of the challenges in front of me.

28. I refuse to let fear cripple my mind from clearly seeing the opportunities I have to overcome the obstacles in my way.

29. Even in the presence of fear, my courage will endure.

30. I am sensitive enough to recognise when to retreat in order to gather more strength and create better strategies for solving my problems.

31. I take my goals seriously and I am committed to achieving every single one of them with sheer determination and faith in myself.

32. I let go of every negative habit or attitude that may stand in the way of my progress in life. I refuse to be an obstacle in my own life.

33. I let go of relationships that may hinder my growth and progress in life.

34. I develop the intelligence to manoeuvre through obstacles.

35. I take active steps to sharpen my problem-solving skills.

36. I take charge or my will and my emotions to subdue outbursts that may cloud my judgement.

37. I learn from past mistakes and I face my challenges with newfound zeal and lessons learnt from past attempts.

38. The colour of my skin is not a limitation, it is an asset that sets me apart for accomplishments.

39. I mute the voices of discouragement in my head and instead I begin to think thoughts and speak words of encouragement over my life.

40. I begin to see and address myself as an overcomer.

41. I am constantly working on myself and therefore the challenges I face are met with a newer and better improved version of myself.

42. I fearlessly handle any and all situations in my life.

43. My resolve to succeed remains unyielding even in the face of adversity.

44. My body responds with tenacity to everything my mind wills it to do.

45. I refuse to be inhibited by any social construct because they do not define me. I decide I far I go on my journey.

46. The greater the obstacle, the greater my celebration when I overcome it.

47. The only obstacle powerful enough to crush my dreams is my inability to try harder therefore I refuse to be my own biggest enemy.

48. Sometimes brilliant opportunities are disguised as impossible situations, I take advantage of every situation and I am rewarded with life changing opportunities.

49. I choose not to complain about difficult situations, instead I uplift my spirit by focusing on how to make the best out of every situation I find myself in.

50. I am a strong, independent and grown, I am capable enough to take care of myself and handle my business.

51. Today I will take the leap of faith to try something I have always been scared to try.

52. I will endure my battles and I will reap the benefits of my endurance.

53. I am equipped with everything I need to go through my experiences with grace and dignity.

54. The obstacles I face today are not big enough to drown my future in discouragement.

55. I will continue to build my resilience to tackle every challenge that comes my way.

56. I will be patient with myself through the process of solving and overcoming my problems.

57. I trust in my abilities and determination to carry me over the obstacles in my way.

58. My challenges are not as difficult as they seem, I will not be intimidated by their appearance.

59. I am an overcomer and my experiences in life will bear witness to that fact.

60. I am tougher than I seem and my life will reflect that there is more to me than meets the eye.

61. My mind is brilliant and it offers me brilliant solutions to overcome whatever obstacle may stand in my way.

62. I give myself space to relax and breathe whenever I feel overwhelmed with anxiety.

63. My mind and body work together to assist me in gaining victory over all of life's trials and disappointments.

64. With faith in myself, my ability to conquer my challenges is limitless.

65. I will pick myself up and face the fears that have defeated me in the past.

66. I will not be intimidated into backing down from whatever challenge stands in the way of my goal.

67. I have set out to conquer my fears and fulfil my destiny, I will not return discouraged and defeated.

68. I do not need to be anybody else to make my dreams a reality, I have everything I need within me.

69. Though life's challenges may be tempting, I will not compromise my principles or boundaries.

70. I will not give into the pressure of coveting other people's achievement, instead I will focus my energy on my own success story in the making.

71. I am able to take my mind off the immediate problem to visualise the bigger picture of success.

72. I possess the grace to surmount even the most difficult hurdles in life that others have tried and fail.

73. The goal is to succeed at everything that I endeavour, failure is not an option.

74. I might make mistakes but I will never quit.

75. I use my past mistakes to my advantage.

76. I trust that in everything that I do, I have a support system that has my back.

77. Being a man of colour neither makes me too weak nor underqualified to accomplish my goals.

78. I have faith that even the obstacles that I face are there to develop my character and teach me endurance because everything works together for my good.

79. I can do all things because I draw my strength from an endless supply.

80. I do not struggle blindly, I run my race with dexterity and a sound mind.

81. As gold is purified by going through the fire, I will go through my adversity and come out stronger and better.

82. I have the ability to conquer all things through persistence and a positive mind set.

83. I will be continually strengthened through my efforts and resolve to never give up on myself.

84. I am strong enough to take whatever life throws at me and I am resourceful enough to use them to my advantage.

85. I am brave enough to step out of the unfavourable circumstances around me, I dare to do better with my life.

86. I refuse to let impatience rob me of the benefits of all my hard work, I will continue to press on.

87. My little victories are worth celebrating, they prepare me for the bigger ones ahead.

88. Even though good things hardly come easy, I will give whatever it takes to get the best of things in my life.

89. My mistakes make me more familiar with my adversity and I discover how to defeat it by learning from my mistakes.

90. All of my problems have solutions and that means they are not impossible to for me to overcome.

91. I am not a failure, my challenges do not define me.

92. I will patiently endure my pain in order to enjoy the gain that comes with it.

93. My difficult journey will lead me to a place of beauty and rest.

94. I let go of hesitation and I find my way through, around, over or under all obstacles that try to hinder my progress.

95. I shake off all doubts about myself and my journey as I step decidedly into action to accomplish my biggest dreams.

96. I may restart my journey as many times as I need to in order refocus and readjust, but I will never give up.

97. I possess a brilliant mind capable of breaking down complex situations into simplicities that can easily be overcome.

98. I have a dynamic personality that can approach any challenge from different angles in order to find the best solution for solving it.

99. Whenever fear tries to overwhelm me, I look deep within to find strength and I transform my fears into the energy that propels me forward on my journey.

Conclusion

So, there you have it. You have reached the end of the 365 affirmations. I hope you are feeling as powerful as I did whilst writing them. You have a voice that will be heard. You have strength that will be seen. You have drive that will succeed. Never forget that.

Revisit these affirmations whenever you can feel any self-doubt or negativity creeping back in. Do not worry about the way you are feeling. My dad always used to tell me, *"worrying is like sitting on a rocking chair; it gives you something to do, but doesn't get you anywhere"*.

Please leave a review if you have enjoyed 365 Positive Affirmations for Black Men. It would be extremely appreciated, and will encourage other men to take the next step in finding positivity.

Printed in Great Britain
by Amazon

50127613R00030